# INTO THE CAULDRON

## The Lancaster MK.I
## Daylight Raid on Augsburg
## 17 April 1942

Hugh Harkins

ISBN: 1-903630-55-X
ISBN-13: 978-1-903630-55-6

# Into The Cauldron
## The Lancaster MK.I
## Daylight Raid on Augsburg
## 17 April 1942

© Hugh Harkins 2015

Published by Centurion Publishing
United Kingdom

ISBN 10: 1-903630-55-X
ISBN 13: 978-1-903630-55-6

This volume first published in 2015

The Publisher and Author would like to thank all organisations and services for
their assistance and contributions in the preparation of this volume

# CONTENTS

# INTRODUCTION

The aim of this volume is to provide a comprehensive study of Operation Margin, the audacious daylight raid on the M.A.N. (Maschinenfabrik Augsburg Nürnberg) Diesel Engine Works in Augsburg, Bavaria, by Avro Lancaster MK.I Bombers of No.44 and 97 Squadrons, No.5 Group, RAF Bomber Command, which was conducted on 17 April 1942.

The volume covers Bomber Commands operational situation leading up to April 1942 and a brief description of the Lancaster MK.I bomber and its initial fielding with No.44 and 97 Squadrons, but it is not intended to be a monograph on the Lancaster itself.

The mission is described in detail, including aircrew, weapons carried, weapons dropped by each aircraft that reached the target and the combats with German fighters en-route to the target.

The volume is supported by a wealth of operational documents including Combat Reports and Squadron Narratives In some cases spelling of specific places or names, timings and numbers and types of enemy aircraft encountered may vary as operational documents, some of which are reproduced verbatim, contradict each other.

# 1

# BOMBER COMMAND AND THE LANCASTER MK.I

When Britain entered World War II on 3 September 1939, the Royal Air Force bomber force consisted of a variety of light, medium and heavy bombers in the shape of the Single-engine Fairey Battle light bombers. twin engine Bristol Blenheim medium bombers and twin engine Handley Page Hampden, Armstrong Whitworth Whitley and Vickers Wellington heavy bombers. Up to summer 1940 the day and night bomber operations of both Germany and Britain had been restrained, with a few exceptions, being restricted to targets that could be easily justified as military in nature or support.

During the German invasion of France and the Low Countries in May and June 1940, the major focus of the Luftwaffe was on providing tactical support to its armies in the field, while the bomber forces, tactical in composition, were mainly focused on targeting infrastructure considered vital to the German offensive. It was during the intensive air battles of May 1940 that the RAF learned the painful lesson that its bombers were extremely vulnerable to enemy fighters and ground defenses when conducting large scale daylight operations. As losses mounted the RAF increasingly turned towards night bombing, although daylight bombing would continue on a reduced scale.

As the period known as the Battle of Britain was nearing its end approaching winter 1940, the Germans too, at the end of a summer of heavy losses in aircraft and crews, turned more towards night bombing, although, like the British, they too would continue daylight bombing on a smaller scale than before.

An Island nation, reliant on the sea for its very survival, much of Britain's bomber offensive had been geared towards attacks on naval targets and naval infrastructure in accordance with the wishes of the Admiralty, heavily embroiled in the Battle of the Atlantic. Since the dark days of summer 1940, when Britain faced a very real threat of invasion, the bomber offensive had been conducted mainly by night; the light bombers of No.2 Group Bomber Command flying daylight raids on continental fringe targets, firstly as an anti-invasion measure and then as part of the overall air offensive over the continent, whereby large formations of British fighters would fly cover for small formations of Bristol Blenheim IV bombers. In these operations, termed Circus's, the bombers in effect acted as bait to lure Luftwaffe fighters up to intercept whereby the German fighters could be engaged by the large formations of British fighters, the first such operation being flown on 14 January 1941.

While No.2 Group flew the bulk of Bomber Commands daylight sorties other Groups were tasked with such raids on a smaller scale.

**Augsburg had been raided before, notably during Bomber Commands early offensive against Germany. Whitley MK.V N1382 DY-A of No.102 Squadron was lost during a raid against Augsburg on the night of 16/17 August 1940. The aircraft, in the background, is seen earlier in the year at Driffield.** MOI

In contrast with summer 1940 when the RAF had faced the bulk of the Luftwaffe bomber and fighter forces, the German presence in France and the Low Countries had been much reduced as Germany had turned East, launching Operation Barbarossa, the invasion of the Soviet Union, on 22 June 1941. Smaller numbers of German units had also been diverted to the Balkans and Mediterranean Theatres. At home, the a major role for Bomber and Fighter

Commands was in effect to attempt to tie down as many German air units in Western Europe as possible in order to assist the Soviets in their titanic struggle for survival as they faced the German onslaught. In this they were not entirely successful, the Luftwaffe for example holding the Channel Front with only two Jagdgeschwader, JG 2 and JG 26. Only a token German bomber force was retained in the west, capable of little more than nuisance raids, with the occasional short duration heavier offensive, but no longer capable of mounting offensives on the scale of those of 1940. In fact, it would not be inaccurate to state that the Germans had, with a token force, succeeded in tying down the bulk of the RAF's fighter and bomber assets at home, whereas more units could have been sent to the Middle and Far East theatres where they were sorely needed. This of course is only part of the picture. In summer 1941, and to a lesser degree in 1942, Britain still had the threat of invasion to cope with, necessitating the retention of superior air forces at home.

Going into 1941, the introduction of the new generation of British heavy bombers was underway, the first of these being the Short Stirling, the first of the RAF's four-engine heavy bombers. A half scale prototype had conducted its maiden flight in September 1938, followed by the full scale prototype, which flew in May 1939. Deliveries of production aircraft commenced to No.7 Squadron in August 1940. The first casualties were six aircraft destroyed on the production line during a Luftwaffe bombing raid.

The Stirling flew its first operational mission on the night of 10/11 February 1941, when No.7 Squadron bombed Rotterdam in The Netherlands. While the aircraft was urgently required for the bomber offensive, it was handicapped with a poor operational ceiling and load carrying capability, the operational units being not overly enthusiastic about it.

Following not far behind the Stirling, the Avro 679 Manchester, which was designed to meet Specification P.13/36, was a twin-engine heavy bomber capable of carrying loads of 8,000 lb., the prototype flying on 25 July 1939. Production aircraft were delivered to No.207 Squadron from November 1940, and the aircraft conducted its first operational bombing sorties when a force attacked the port of Brest, France, on the night of 24/25 February 1941. For the most part the aircraft design was sound, but problems with the Rolls Royce Vulture engines led to it being superseded by the Avro Lancaster after only 209 aircraft had been delivered, production ending in November 1941.

The third of the initial trio of new heavy bomber designs was the Handley Page Halifax. The first production Halifax MK.I, L9485, conducted its maiden flight on 11 October 1940, and deliveries to Bomber Command commenced when No.35 Squadron began receiving Halifax MK.I bombers in November that year, operational missions being flown from March 1941.

**Prior to the introduction of the Lancaster, many daylight raids had been conducted by heavy bombers of Bomber Command, although none had penetrated as deep into enemy territory as Augsburg. Here Halifax bombers from No.35 Squadron are targeting the German Battlecruisers *Scharnhorst* and *Gneisenau* in dry dock at Brest, France, on 18 December 1941.** RAF

Following the introduction of the Halifax a number of daylight bombing missions were flown. The first of these being a daylight attack on the German port of Kiel, conducted by six Halifax I bombers from No.35 Squadron on 30 June 1941; two of the bombers being lost. As the summer of 1941 wore on Halifax bombers, along with other bombers of Bomber Command, including the Short Stirling, would also be employed on daylight attacks on the German warships in the French port of Brest.

"You will direct the main effort of the bomber force, until further instructions, towards dislocating the German transportation system, and to destroying the moral of the civil population as a whole, and of the industrial workers in particular". This was the directive issued to Air Marshal Sir Richard Peirse, Commander in Chief of Bomber Command on 9 July 1941. When this directive was issued Bomber Command consisted of 49 Squadrons (some documents adjust this figure slightly depending on the operational status of some squadrons), made up of, for the most part, Hamden, Whitley and

4

Wellington twin engine medium bombers (these types had been re-designated from heavy to medium bombers with the introduction of later heavy types). There were eight Squadrons of the new heavy bombers, four being operational, and eight Squadrons of Bristol Blenheim's, now classified as a light bomber, operating with No.2 Group in the daylight bombing role. The thirty seven available medium and heavy bomber squadrons were tasked with night bombing in accordance with the directive issued on 9 July 1941, but some daylight attacks were launched The eight Blenheim Squadrons would continue daylight attacks on continental fringe and shipping targets, operating from medium and low altitudes, often heavily protected by fighters, occasionally venturing further afield to attack targets in Germany. Absent from the above figures was No.90 Squadron with its Boeing Fortress MK.I's (B-17C), which would be employed in an experimental high altitude bombing role, which, despite the directive of 9 July, would be conducted mainly against naval targets and port towns, as would much of Bomber Commands night bomber offensive.

Throughout 1941 and the first months of 1942, Bomber Command's main preoccupation continued to be area bombing under the cover of darkness. There were of course daylight operations as noted above, mainly by the light bombers of No.2 Group, and, on a smaller scale, by the medium and heavy bombers of the Command, particularly against strategically important targets such as the German Battlecruisers at Brest.

The night bombing offensive had been, for the most part, inaccurate, many crews unable to find the targets in the pitch blackness and often adverse weather conditions found over North West Europe. Improvements to the capability of bombers employed in the night offensive against Germany would include the deployment of GEE, development of which commenced in 1940 under R.J. Dippy of the Telecommunications Research Establishment. This in effect calculated the position of an aircraft by determining the time it took to receive "pulse signals" emitted by three separate ground stations on the East coast of England. Initially operations were flown with a "few hand-made sets" during the second half of 1941, but it was not until February 1942 that sufficient GEE set boxes were available for a proper operational deployment. In order to conserve aircraft Bomber Command, in November 1941, had reduced the tempo of operations in preparation for a new more accurate offensive against Germany, planned for early 1942 using GEE, but it was recognized that GEE had its limitations, range being only around 300 miles, which limited the targets that could be bombed using the new technology. In addition, it was recognised that GEE was not a precision bombing aid, rather it was an aid to put bombers in the general area of the target accurately under the cover of darkness; Bomber Command would still be employed mainly in area bombing. Precision strikes against high value targets could only be conducted during daylight hours with all the inherent risks that this involved.

The Lancaster was developed from the Avro 679 Manchester bomber, which was powered by two Rolls Royce Vulture engines. The Manchester could easily be distinguished from the later Lancaster by its twin-engine arrangement and dorsal fin ahead of the tail turret. RAF

**No.44 (Rhodesia) Squadron was the first Squadron to become operational with Lancaster's. Early missions included minelaying and bombing over Northern Germany. This vic of three Lancaster's of 44 Squadron was photographed from an aircraft of another Section.** RAF

On 20 February 1942, Air Marshal Arthur T. Harris succeeded Sir Richard Peirse as the Commander-in-Chief of Bomber Command, based at RAF High Wycombe. On the 14th of the month Bomber Command had been instructed to "strike with full force for the next six months", the reduced tempo of operations was at an end. That same month records show that Bomber Command's main strength consisted of 49 Squadrons, including five Squadrons of light bombers of No.2 Group. Of the remaining 44 Squadrons, thirty eight of which were operational, fourteen were equipped with heavy bombers, Stirling's, Manchester's and Halifax's, the rest being equipped with a variety of medium bomber types - Wellington, Whitley and Hampden. The Fortress I high altitude bombers had been withdrawn from the daylight bombing role and transferred to Coastal Command, a few going to North Africa. No.44 Squadron was about to become operational on the Lancaster MK.I and No.97 Squadron was commencing conversion to the new heavy bomber. Although Squadron numbers were about the same as they had been in mid-1941, the Commands bomb carrying capability had increased enormously with the conversion of more Squadrons to the four engine heavies.

The Lancaster had a cavernous bomb bay in comparison to previous generation bombers. The aircraft was the true big lifter of the war, capable of carrying larger bomb loads and bombs of larger size than any other aircraft of its generation. Although the bomb bay could accommodate 14 x 1,000 lb. bombs, the distance to be flown at low level on Operation Margin dictated that each aircraft would carry only 4 such weapons. RAF

**The cockpit of a Lancaster MK.I showing control panels and flying controls.** BO

The Avro Type 683 Lancaster prototype, serial BT308, initially known as the Manchester III, was a conversion of a twin-engine Avro Manchester bomber fitted with 4 x Rolls Royce Merlin X engines. This aircraft, which retained the Manchester's tail assembly, including the central fin, conducted its maiden flight at Woodford on 9 January 1941, before the Manchester had commenced operations. The aircraft conducted acceptance trials at the A&AEE., Bascombe Down, Wiltshire, in late January 1941. Later the tail assembly was altered, the central fin being removed and a new twin fin arrangement installed on a 33 ft. span tail plane. A new build prototype, DG585, conducted its maiden flight on 13 May 1941, and the first production Lancaster MK.I bomber, L7527, conducted its maiden flight at Woodford on 31 October that year.

The Lancaster had a huge bomb bay, a tremendous load carrying ability and adequate performance for a heavy bomber of the time, and would go on, together with the Halifax, to be a stalwart of Bomber Commands strength until the end of the war in 1945; 7,734 Lancaster's of all models being built.

The Lancaster MK.I was powered by four Rolls Royce Merlin XX engines fitted with SU carburetors. The engines drove hydromantic propellers and burned 100 octane fuel which was fed to the engines by three self-sealing fuel tanks in each wing; locations being No.1 (Inner) housed between the fuselage and the inner Merlin engines, No.2 (Centre) located between the engines and No.3 (Outer) located outboard of the outer engines. The No.1 tanks each housed 580 gallons, the No.2 tanks each housed 383 gallons and the No.3 tanks each housed 114 gallons for a combined total of 2,154 gallons. Fuel capacity could be increased in some aircraft equipped to carry either one or two 400 gallon auxiliary fuel tanks in the bomb bay. The auxiliary tanks fed into the No.1 wing tanks as these emptied, thence onward to feed the engines.

The Lancaster I had a maximum speed of 280 plus mph and an operating altitude of some 20,000 ft., depending on aircraft conditions and weights. Generally the Lancaster climbed at a recommended speed of 160 mph I.A.S. Flying at normal speeds and loadings the Lancaster had a "satisfactory" stability up to about 67,000 lb., but at loadings above this there was "a tendency for the aircraft to wallow", which could be further aggravated by use of flight controls to try and correct the wallow.

**Cutaway of the Lancaster MK.I as it was presented in 1942.** MAP

Described as being "relatively light and effective" the elevators could become "heavy" when the aircraft was in a turn. The ailerons were "light and effective", but at speeds above 260 m.p.h I.A.S. and when the aircraft was operating at heavy loads, they became "heavy".

In a high speed dive the aircraft became nose heavy and the standard doctrine was for the flight engineer to be available to assist the pilot as required, particularly in the pull out.

Stalling speeds at 50,000 lb. weight were 95 m.p.h. I.A.S. with undercarriage and flaps up, and 83 m.p.h. I.A.S. with undercarriage and flaps down. Typical recommended approach speeds for the aircraft at a weight of 45,000 lb. was 110 m.p.h I.A.S. under power.

Considered the primary defensive armament, the tail turret housed 4 x .303 in Browning machine guns. The Lancaster I was also had two such weapons in the nose dorsal and ventral turrets, the later eventually being removed. RAF

**This Lancaster BMK.I, R5727, on the ramp at Prestwick, Scotland, in August 1942, was the first Lancaster to fly across the Atlantic when it was flown to Canada to be used as the pattern for Lancaster production in that country.** MAP

Operating Handley Page Hampdens in the first few years of the war, No.44 (Rhodesia) Squadron (the Squadron received the Rhodesia title in 1941) began receiving production Lancaster MK.I's towards the end of 1941, allowing air and ground crew to commence proper training on the type. Lancaster prototype BT308 had apparently been used by the Squadron for familiarisation training as far back as September 1941. The obsolete Hampdens were withdrawn from December 1941, the Squadron concentrating on working up with the new Lancaster bombers during January 1942, training continuing through February and into March that year. The first operational mission with the Lancaster was flown on 3 March 1942, a 'Gardening' mission, mines being dropped in the Heligoland Bight in the North Sea close to the German coast.

In May 1940, No.97 Squadron reformed as an operational unit in No.4 Group operating Whitley bombers from Driffield, but this was short lived and the unit was disbanded that same month. The Squadron reformed at Waddington in February 1941, equipped with Avro Manchester Heavy bombers within No.5 Group, moving to Coningsby in April 1941 for operations over Europe. In January 1942, the Squadron began converting to Avro Lancaster MK.I bombers.

2

# THE AUGSBURG RAID

In the weeks following his appointment as Commander-in-Chief of Bomber Command, Air Marshal Harris, although accepting that the bulk of Bomber Commands effort against Germany would have to be conducted under the cover of darkness, began planning an audacious long-range precision bombing mission that would penetrate deep into Germany in broad daylight, thus was born Operation Margin. Without consulting the Air Ministry, or the Ministry of Economic Warfare, Harris settled on the M.A.N. (Maschinenfabrik Augsburg Nürnberg)) Diesel Engine Works located in Augsburg in Bavaria.

Harris decided to utilise his newest bomber type, the Avro Lancaster MK.I, which had just become operational with No.44 and 97 Squadrons at RAF Waddington and Woodhall Spa respectively, each Squadron providing one Flight of six aircraft each for the mission. Crews were taken off normal operations to conduct low level daylight flying training for the operation.

No.44 Squadron was commanded by twenty five year old S/Ldr. John. Derring Nettleton, a relatively inexperienced first tour pilot from South Africa. He had joined the RAF in 1938 and by the time of Operation Margin had flown only 15 operational sorties. No.97 Squadron was commanded by twenty three year old S/Ldr. John Seymour Sherwood who had been awarded a DFC during his first tour. He had previously flown daylight operations, notably a mission against the German Battlecruisers *Scharnhorst* and *Gneisenau*.at Brest.

On the morning of 11 April 1942, No.44 Squadron had only two Lancaster's serviceable out of its establishment of eighteen aircraft. It was on this date that the Squadron was informed it was to conduct daytime formation flying with two sections, each of three aircraft. At this time the planned operation was kept secret from crews, who were informed that the flights had the purpose of "flying a long distance to obtain data on the endurance of Lancaster Aircraft under formation flying conditions."

**Map of Europe showing the British Isles, France and Germany, the principal
operating areas of Bomber Command. Augsburg (not on map) near Nürnberg
(Nuremberg) was the distant target chosen for Operation Margin.** NZTEC

**No.44 Squadron Lancaster MK.I L7575/KM-B, flown by S/Ldr. Nettleton, flies east to west across RAF Waddington with bomb bay doors open during a practice sortie for Operation Margin.** RAF

On the morning of the 12th, only four Lancaster's were serviceable, this reducing to two aircraft by 18.00 hours. 'B' Flight continued flying training. Only two aircraft were serviceable on the morning of the 13th, this increasing to seven by late afternoon. Formation flying practice continued with a total of 3.5 hours flown. On the morning of the 14th, aircraft serviceability increased to seven Lancaster's of the seventeen on strength. The low-level formation flying training ramped up with six aircraft flying a total of 10.25 hours in the afternoon.

On the morning of the 15th, aircraft serviceability was kept at seven. No operational flying was scheduled for the Squadron, but what was in effect a dress rehearsal for the coming operation was conducted by six Lancaster's and crews; L7578 (S/Ldr. Nettleton, P/O. Dorehill, P/O. Sands, F/Lt. McClure,

Sgt. Churchill, F/Sgt. Harrison 045, F/Sgt. Mutter and Sgt. Huntly), R5516 (F/O. Garwell, DFM, Sgt. Dando, F/Sgt. Kirke, DFM, Sgt. Edwards 677, F/Sgt. Flux, DFM and P/O. Lovegrove), L7536 (Sgt. Rhodes, Sgt. Baxter, Sgt. Daly, Sgt. Merricks and Sgt. Wynton), R5506 (F/Sgt. Sandford, P/O. Peall, F/O. Gerrie, Sgt. Hadgraft, Sgt. Ventor, F/Sgt. Law and Sgt. Wing), L7581 (W/O. Crum, DFM, Sgt. Dedman, Sgt. Birkett, F/Sgt. Sanderson, Sgt. Miller, Sgt. Dowty and Sgt. Cobb) and L7584 (W/O. Beckett, DFM, Sgt. Moss, F/Sgt. Ross, Sgt. Seagoe, Sgt. Hacket, Sgt. Harrison 678 and Sgt. Trustram).

The days training operation was a planned flight along the route "Base (Waddington) - Selsey Bill – Lincoln – Falkirk – Inverness – Falkirk – Base" Inverness in the north of Scotland was the target for the exercise, but the crews were briefed to only approach the outskirts and not to fly directly over the town. Minimum altitude for this exercise was set at 500 ft., lower than any of the previous training flights. The two formations of three aircraft each were led by S/Ldr. Nettleton and F/Lt. Sandford respectively. Nettleton's Section flew a round distance of 1,020 miles in 5 hours and 25 minutes, while Sanford's Section covered a round distance of 1,014 miles in 5 hours and 30 minutes.

Preparations with 97 Squadron at Woodhall Spa included formation flying on the 11th. On the 12th, the Squadron had eight aircraft serviceable, six of these being allocated for more formation flying training, however, only four aircraft participated as two "were unable to take off". Formation flying continued on the 13th, six aircraft and two reserves being allocated for the program. The aircraft were loaded with 4 x 1,000 lb. dummy bombs and 4 x 11.5 lb. practice bombs. The six Lancaster's, led by S/Ldr. Sherwood, flew "a cross country" and practice bombed Wainfleet. The following day eight Lancaster's again practice bombed Wainfleet and a formation exercise was flown lasting 5 to 5.5 hours. Practice bombing of Wainfleet was again conducted on the 15th, and or the 16th (records are unclear), with a "short cross country" flight training exercise flown on the 16th.

During one training flight F/O. Rodley noticed the radio mast at Rugby ahead of the aircraft. He was sure the leading vic had not noticed the mast due to misty conditions. Despite orders for radio silence a concerned Rodley decided he would call out the masts, but this was rendered unnecessary as he immediately saw the six leading Lancaster's go into a violent climb to which they were in almost 'plan view' from Rodney's position.

The planned raid itself had a number of stated objectives. Primarily, like so many of the daylight raids by RAF heavy bombers, it was part of the wider Battle of the Atlantic. Second it was aimed at showing the enemy that the RAF had the capability to strike right into the heart of Germany in broad daylight, hopefully necessitating him to disperse his fighter forces and retain additional units, which otherwise could be employed on the Eastern Front or Mediterranean Theatre, for home defence against any future enterprise by the

RAF in daylight hours. The raid would also test the capabilities of the new Lancaster heavy bomber which had only just commenced operations the previous month.

The plan seemed straightforward; twelve Lancaster bombers would cross the French coast at low level to avoid detection by enemy radar, "penetrate deep into France", flying at 500 ft. or lower until south of Paris, then on a course that would feint for Munich in Southern Bavaria before the aircraft turned northward towards Augsburg, the target being attacked with 1,000 lb. bombs set with 11 second delayed action fuses.

No fighter escort was to be provided into France as this, it was thought, would draw unnecessary attention to the raiding force. Instead, a number of diversionary bombing operations and fighter sweeps were to be conducted in the Pas de Calais, Cherbourg and Rouen areas with some 800 fighter and fighter bomber sorties and a smaller number of bomber sorties by Douglas Boston light bombers of No.2 Group. This, it was hoped, would draw the German fighter force up and occupy them; they, it was hoped, being either otherwise engaged with the diversionary operations or refueling and rearming, therefore leaving the Lancaster force unmolested.

Throughout the night of 16 April and the morning and early afternoon of the 17th, the aircraft were prepared at Waddington and Woodhall Spa for the coming operation. Seven Lancaster's (six for the operation and 1 reserve) were prepared at both stations. Each aircraft carrying 2,154 gallons of 100 octane aviation fuel and armed with a bomb load of 4 x 1,000 lb. bombs with 11 second delay fuses.

The briefing was conducted in the early afternoon of Friday, 17 April (note some accounts state the briefing took place at 11.00 am, however, all operational records clearly state the briefing took place in the early afternoon). Prior to the briefing the Section Leaders had been told what the target was. Apparently when the curtain covering the huge wall map in the briefing room was pulled away at the 97 Squadron briefing at Woodhall Spa, the route to Augsburg clearly marked out in red ribbon, there was a sudden burst of laughter from the crews, many of whom assumed it was a prank of some kind. It is often stated in contemporary accounts that this was due to the fact that the RAF had never flown raids that far into Germany before at night, let alone in daylight. However, this is inaccurate, the RAF having previously flown raids against Augsburg as far back as summer 1940. For example Whitley's bombed Augsburg on the night of 16/17 August 19140 as part of Bomber Commands early offensive against Germany. Miffed at the behavior of some of the aircrew, the crews were brought into line by the senior officers as the briefing progressed. At Waddington the atmosphere was rather more somber as the crews contemplated the mission to come. The crews were shown photographs of the target, and, at Woodhall Spa at least, a model of the MAN works.

**Lancaster MK.I L7575/KM-B casts a shadow as it flies over British fields during a practice low level sortie on 14 April 1942. The training flights were restricted to altitudes above 500 ft., higher than the altitude that would be employed on Operation Margin.** RAF

As stated above, on paper the plan seemed straightforward: the Lancaster's would takeoff from their respective bases before loosely forming up later to cross the English Channel, cross the French coast near Deauville, continue across France before turning onto an easterly course south of Paris, continue towards Lake Constance when the formation would swing north east towards Ammersee, Bavaria and feint towards Munich before swinging north to attack Augsburg. The mission would involve a flight of almost 500 miles into enemy territory. The crews were briefed that they didn't have to worry about the heavy anti-aircraft guns such as the 88 mm's as they could not fire at aircraft operating that low, this of course being inaccurate, although it was certainly true that such guns would have a very limited time to be brought to bear, vastly reducing their effectiveness against very low flying aircraft.

There was a real concern among aircrew over small arms coming up through the bottom of the aircraft and through the seats, resulting in many of the crews, particularly from 97 Squadron, getting pieces of armour plate from the armoury, which were laid on the seats. At least one crew member who didn't get armour plate apparently sat on an old steel helmet, certainly the ingredients for an extremely uncomfortable flight.

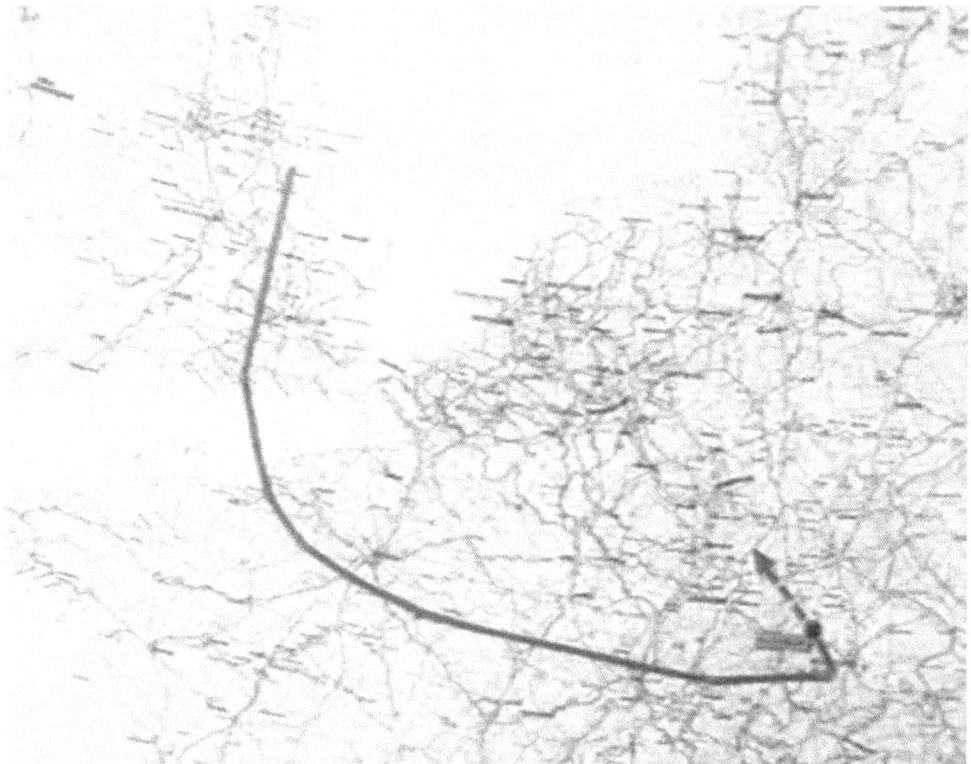

The mission got underway at 14.55 hours on the afternoon of 17 April 1942 when the first of No.97 Squadrons aircraft, L7573/K (S/Ldr. Sherwood, DFC, P/O. Webb, F/O. Hepburn, Sgt. Page, Sgt. Cox, F/Sgt. Harrington and F/Sgt. Wilding), lifted off from Woodhall Spa. Around one minute later R5537/B (F/O. Hallows, P/O. Friend, P/O. Cutting, F/Sgt. Lough, Sgt. Jones, L.G., Sgt. Broomfield and Sgt. Goacher), took off, followed at 14.57 hours by R5488/F (F/O. Rodley, P/O. Colquhoun, Sgt. Henley, Sgt. Merralls, Sgt. Cummings, Sgt. Ratcliffe and Sgt. Crisp). These aircraft were then joined by the second formation of three Lancaster's which commenced take off at 14.58 hours when R5496/U (F/Lt. Penman, DFC, 2nd formation leader, P/O. Hooey, P/O. Ifoulds, F/Sgt. Elwood, Sgt. Tales, Sgt. Overton and Sgt. Hebdon) lifted off. This was followed into the air by L7575/Y (F/O. Deverill, DFM, Sgt. Cooper, P/O. Butlery, Sgt. Irons, Sgt. Mackay, Sgt. Devine and F/Sgt. Keane), and lastly R5513/P (W/O. Mycock, DFM, Sgt. Hayes, W/O. Harrison, Sgt. Eades, Sgt. Macdonald, Sgt. Shelly and Sgt. Donaghue) lifting off at 15.00 hours.

Sherwood led the first vic with Eric Rodley on his right wing and Hallows on his left wing. F/Lt David Penman led the second vic with 22 year old W/O. Mycock on his right wing and F/O. Deverill on his left wing.

For 44 Squadron at Waddington, the mission got underway at 15.12 hours when the six Lancaster's, R5508/B (S/Ldr. Nettleton, P/O. Dorehill, P/O. Sands, F/Lt. McClure, Sgt. Churchill, Sgt. Huntley, F/Sgt. Mutter and F/Sgt.

Harrison), R5510/A (F/O. Garwell, DFM, Sgt. Dando, F/Sgt. Kirke, DFM, F/Sgt. Flux, DFM, Sgt. Watson, F/Sgt. Edwards and F/Sgt. McAlpinne), L7536/H (Sgt. Rhodes, Sgt. Baxter, Sgt. Daly, Sgt. Merricks, Sgt. Wynton, F/Sgt. Edwards and F/Sgt. Gill), L7565/V (W/O. Beckett, DFM, Sgt. Moss, F/Sgt. Rees, Sgt. Seagoe, Sgt. Hacket, Sgt. Harrison and Sgt. Trustram), R5506/P (F/Lt. Sandford, DFC, P/O. Peall, F/O. Gerrie, Sgt. Hadgraft, Sgt. Venter, F/Sgt. Law and Sgt. Wing) and L7548/T (W/O. Crum, DFM, Sgt. Dedman, Sgt. Birkett, F/Sgt. Sanderson, Sgt. Miller, Sgt. Dowty and Sgt. Cobb), began lifting off from Waddington. Nettleton led the first vic with Sandford leading the second vic. Setting take off for mid-afternoon was designed to enable the aircraft to make the major part of the return journey under the cover of darkness.

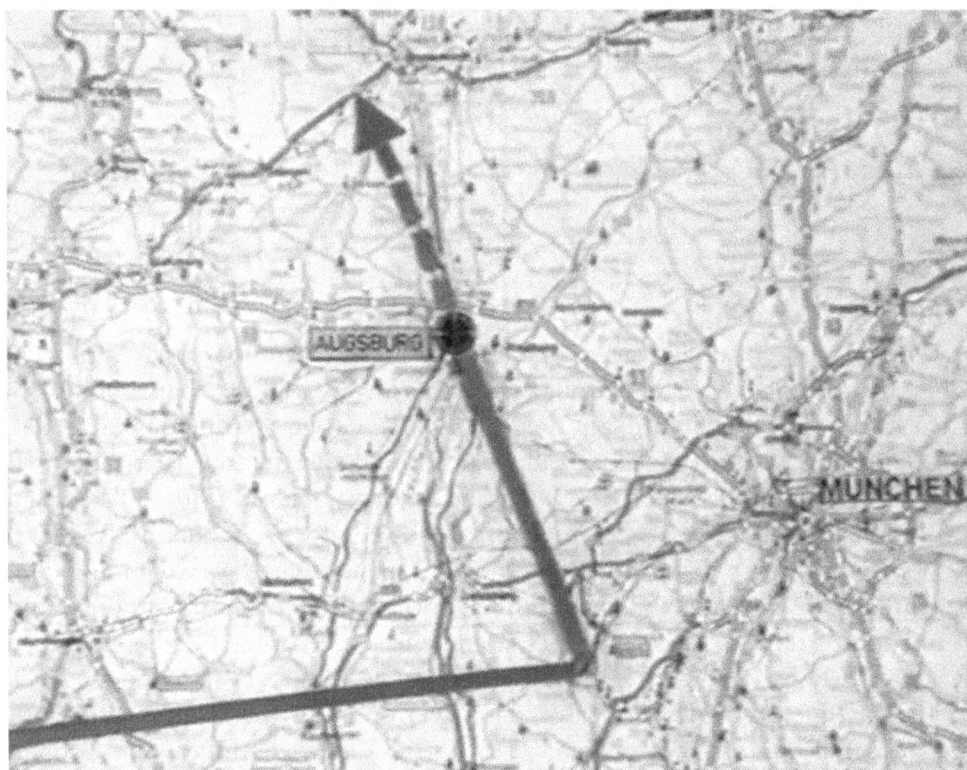

**Previous page: This map is understood to be a copy of the original briefing map showing the Lancaster route from Lincolnshire to Augsburg. The twelve Lancaster's would cross the English Channel al low level to avoid detection by German radar, cross the French coast, then, when south of Paris, they would set an easterly course before swinging north easterly to feint towards Munich, Bavaria and then turn north towards Augsburg. This page: A close up view of the final legs of the planned flight towards Augsburg, showing the planned withdrawal to the north.**

Prior to take off of the Lancaster formations, the aircraft tasked with the diversionary raids and sweeps had taken off to conduct their respective parts in the operation. This included a patrol of around 100 or so Spitfire fighters over Calais. The Boston light bombers of No.2 Group were allocated targets to be bombed on both sides of the route over the French coast to be taken by the Lancaster's. These operations appear to have been hastily prepared and, perhaps, ill though out, particularly in regards to timings, for the diversion raids only served to bring up formations of German fighters which would still be in a position to intercept when the Lancaster's came over. The official history states "Unfortunately the diversions were not wholly successful: they served to alert rather than distract the defences in France."

The official report to the War Cabinet states "Fighter Command despatched 653 aircraft over Northern France.... the largest number of fighters so far despatched on offensive operations on one day. The majority of these aircraft escorted Boston's and Hurricane Bombers in their attack on land targets." The same report states that 44 bombers were flown on the operations, attacking "a shell factory at Marquise; the docks at Cherbourg; and a Power Station, fuel cisterns and a 300-foot merchant vessel at Grand Quevilly (Rouen)." During these operations one Boston was shot down.

Of the large number of fighter sorties, 15 Squadrons of Spitfires "were engaged in two sweeps over the Cherbourg Peninsula and Pas de Calais, but very little opposition was encountered." During the course of the days operations Fighter Command claimed three German fighters destroyed, one probably destroyed and one damaged. German claims were four Spitfires shot down, but British records confirm only two Spitfires were lost, German losses also being lower than claimed by the RAF.

In the original plan the 44 and 97 Squadron formations should have remained loosely together until near the target when they would separate, each formation then attacking the target independently of each other. However, Sherwood, leading the 97 Squadron formation, apparently thought that the 44 Squadron formation was slightly north of the planned route. Sherwood decided to follow the course he was assured by his navigator was correct with the effect that both formations gradually separated, losing sight of each other either before or shortly after crossing the French coast.

The two formations crossed the French coast east of Caen, the first, the 44 Squadron formation, at around 16.45 hours. The 44 Squadron formation seemed to fly lower than that of 97 Squadron, with reports of aircraft going as low as twenty or thirty feet, although it was unlikely that the aircraft went this low, 50 feet or so being more probable. In any case there are reports that some aircraft had to climb to avoid large trees.

The official history states "Five minutes after Nettleton and his comrades (the 6 Lancaster's from No.44 Squadron) crossed the French coast they were intercepted by twenty five to thirty German fighters." It goes on to state "The first two sections (the six Lancaster's from No.44 Squadron) bore the brunt of the attack. Four of these six bombers were shot down in a long running fight which lasted a full hour." This would imply, or at least lead the reader to infer that the two sections from No.97 Squadron were also intercepted by the German fighters, which, as born-out by British and German operational records and crew statements, we know was not the case.

From the German side we know that the six Lancaster's of 44 Squadron suddenly appeared over, or along, the perimeter of the German airfield at Beaumont le Roger as elements of JG 2, equipped with Messerschmitt Me.109F single-engine fighters, were preparing to land, having been scrambled earlier in the day to confront the various bomber attacks and fighter sweeps put on as a diversion to the Lancaster raid.

A shout of viermots (heavies) went out and the in-bound German fighters were alerted over the radio, aborting their landing and heading after the bombers. At least one other 109F took off with Major Walter Oesau at the controls.

Apparently Lancaster L7548/T, flown by W/O. Crum, was closest to the perimeter of the airfield, no less than three Me.109's being seen in the process of landing. These fighters aborted their landing and went after the six Lancaster's. According to the 44 Squadron Narrative the first Lancaster shot down was apparently L7536/H, flown by Sgt. Rhodes, which was on Nettleton's starboard wing. During the engagement all of the guns on this aircraft apparently jammed or malfunctioned in some way or other. The aircraft was attacked by two 109's and both port side engines caught fire. It seems that a starboard engine was also set alight, the aircraft being noted to climb slightly before it apparently stalled and plummeted Earthwards, hitting the ground in a near vertical dive, all seven crew being killed. It should be noted that other accounts actually put L7536 as the last of the four Lancaster's to be shot down.

The German fighters now turned on the rear vic of three Lancaster's. L7565/V, flown by W/O. Beckett, crashed into trees on fire after being racked with cannon fire, all of the crew being killed. L7548/T, the Lancaster flown by W/O. Crum, was hit in the fuselage by cannon fire, the port wing also being set on fire. During the attack at least two of the crew (both gunners) were injured. The bombs were apparently jettisoned and Crum then crash landed the aircraft wheels up, apparently crossing three fields before the aircraft came to a halt. Trapped in the wreckage, the nose gunner, Sgt. Dowty, used one of the guns to try and smash through the turret, but just then W/O. Crum appeared brandishing an axe which he used to cut through the turret, the gunner climbing out through the hole. Note: Some accounts suggest that L7548/T was actually the second Lancaster to be shot down, but if the 44 Squadron account is adhered to then it would appear more likely that this aircraft was the third Lancaster shot down, a hypothesis with more support in the records of both sides. All seven crewmembers survived and were taken prisoner.

As the fight continued at ultra-low level, F/Lt. Sandford flew Lancaster R5506/P, the remaining aircraft of the rear vic, ever lower in an attempt to shake off his assailants, apparently three German fighters pursuing him. In the desperate attempt to escape the Lancaster was even apparently flown under high tension cables, but to no avail. Hit by bursts of cannon fire all four engines were afire, the Lancaster then hitting the ground and exploding, the entire crew being killed.

F/O. Ginger Garwell's Lancaster, R5510/A, which was on Nettleton's port wing, was attacked, the starboard wing being badly damaged by cannon and or machine gun fire, but the aircraft survived as the German fighters withdrew low on fuel. There is no information of a direct attack on Nettleton's aircraft, although several reports state that both surviving Lancaster's continued to the target after suffering damage in the engagement with the German fighters. This is contradicted by the Combat Report from Nettleton's aircraft which clearly states that Garwell's Lancaster was damaged, but mentions no damage to Nettleton's aircraft, but does state that the gunners in Nettleton's aircraft engaged German fighters. Of the crews of the four Lancaster's shot down, 21 were killed and seven would be captured.

Available German records suggest that the four Lancaster's were shot down by Stab II./JG 2 (Hptm. Karl-Heinz Greisert), 5./JG 2 (Fw. Otto Pohl), 6./JG 2 (Fw. Alexander Bleymuller) and Stab/JG 2 (Maj Walter Oesau). The German side states that Oesau shot down a Lancaster at 16.55 hours near Le Vieil-Evreux, 6 km ESE of Evreux, Greisert shot down a Lancaster at 17.06 in the area of le Tilleul-Lambert/Eure, Pohl shot down a Lancaster, L7536, at 17.07 near Ormes, 14 km WNW of Evreux, this being credited as the Geschwader's 1,000[th] claimed kill since the war began. Bleymuller shot a Lancaster down near Ormes, 14 km WNW of Evreux, time unclear although records suggest 17.10 hours. At least one account also states that the fourth Lancaster to be shot down was brought down by the Ace Major Perceau, commander of the Richthofen Squadron, and yet another that the fourth Lancaster was brought down by Fw. Ernst Bosseckert. The German records, like those of the British are often contradictory and unclear. It is possible that one or more of these pilots attacked Garwell's aircraft which was only damaged. Only four kill claims appear to have been submitted, which corresponds correctly with the number of aircraft shot down.

In some accounts it is claimed that Maj. Oesau had been banned from operational flying after he had achieved 100 kills, however, this is contradicted by statements that when the bombers flew over the airfield he ran to his 109F, which was always kept at readiness.

Records suggest that one aircraft of Stab/ JG.2 was damaged by return fire from a bomber on 17 April 1942, however, it is unclear if this was an earlier combat with Boston light bombers or in the combat with the Lancaster's, the former being the more probable.

The following No.44 Squadron air combat report is reproduced verbatim:

From     Headquarters, R.A.F. Station, Waddington.

To.       Headquarters, No.5 Group, Grantham.

Date:    18th April, 1942.                                    AT/42/1746

**By Squadron Gunnery Leader**
**Squadron….44.**
**Aircraft…. Lancaster.1.   R5508. "B".        BC/3**
**Date of**
**Operation…17th April, 1942.**

Three Lancaster's in Vic formation whilst on their way to target AUGSBURG, Germany, were attacked by a formation of ME 109's and FW190's.

At approximately 16.55 Hrs. near Bernay, France the formation was flying at 100 ft. when attacked by fighters which were sighted at about 1500 ft. flying in the opposite direction. They immediately turned into the attack coming in at Port Quarter to Astern aiming at the engines, opening fire with Cannon at 700 yds. and breaking away at 400 yds. Rear and mid-upper gunners of formation leader opened fire at 500 yds. and gave bursts until breakaway. Approximately twenty attacks were made. The rear and Mid-upper Gunners gave mutual fire support to the other aircraft. Nose gunner claims to have damaged a FW 190 which attacked from Port Bow and vanished to Starboard bow. The Rear and Mid-upper Gunners claim several E/A possibly damaged, but owing to the number and rapidity of the attacks, they were unable to observe any results.
The Combat lasted 10 to 15 minutes during which the aircraft starboard of the leader was hit and seen to dive into the ground on fire. The Port aircraft had one wing badly damaged but continued to Target.

COMMENT.
     The gunners were at a disadvantage owing to the fact that the Enemy aircraft were using cannon, and never came into real effective range for .303.

Handwritten: **3 Lancaster  30 ME 109's and FW 190's.**

The operational orders called for the mission to be aborted in the event that any of the aircraft were lost en-route to the target. Nettleton, with the first wave of six aircraft decimated – four destroyed and at least one damaged – and unaware of the status of the 97 Squadron formation to his rear, elected to continue with the mission. Therefore, following the running battle with the enemy fighters which lasted around a quarter of an hour (Note: accounts vary in regards to how long the engagement with the German fighters lasted, the Official History and a number of reports to the War Cabinet for example state the duration as an hour, but the 44 Squadron Combat Report and German records suggest strongly that around 15 minutes or so was the more accurate) the two surviving 44 Squadron Lancaster's, with the six 97 Squadron machines trailing some ten minutes behind and slightly further south, continued on to the target for the most part unmolested, for it is stated in the official history that they ran into some "flak over an airfield", although there is no mention of this in the operational records.

When south of Paris the two 44 Squadron Lancaster's had set an easterly course for Bavaria, eventually locating Lake Ammersee. At this point the German defence network assumed that the target was Munich, but now the Lancaster's turned North towards the Lech River, the Munich-Augsburg Railway line having been crossed at Mering, the original plan of flying direct to the target being abandoned as it would involve a bomb run through a number of industrial chimney stacks necessitating an undesirable increase in altitude, the Lancaster's following the Lech River to Augsburg which would now be attacked from an easterly direction with less obstruction from chimneys.

The M.A.N. Factory lay in the north east of Augsburg where the River Lech and River Wertach narrowed towards each other. In Augsburg itself, the town's folk were unsuspecting as they celebrated the last day of the annual carnival. Bands were playing and crowds gathered in the narrow streets of the medieval town. In this part of Germany the war seemed distant indeed, without the regular bombing that northern Germany was experiencing, which had bestowed upon the inhabitants a sense of invulnerability to attack.

From Nettleton's aircraft the target could be clearly seen from about seven miles away. The two Lancaster's approached the town at low level, having achieved more or less complete surprise. Residents of Augsburg heard the noise of aircraft engines and then the large bombers were seen flying very low over a forest. As the air raid sirens sounded the two Lancaster's flew over the town, flying between industrial chimney stacks despite the easterly direction off attack, it being stated that the aircraft swept in so low "that the local anti-aircraft gunners knocked down several chimney pots in attempting to shoot them down". As the Lancaster's flew towards the target, which was easily identified, intense and accurate light anti-aircraft fire arced through the sky, although it was later reported that the majority of the heavy flak was relatively inaccurate, the gunners having only fleeting seconds to bring their guns to bear.

At 19.55 hours, the two Lancaster's each released 4 x 1,000 lb. bombs from an altitude of "50 feet". Bombs were noted to burst on target by the rear gunner in Nettleton's aircraft, and by Nettleton himself as the aircraft turned on leaving the target area taking violent evasive manoeuvres, withdrawing in a southerly direction, one of the gunners on Nettleton's aircraft, Sgt. Huntly, opening fire and claiming to have silenced "one of the main defensive gun posts". Large segments of the buildings "blasted into the air" as the bombs detonated. Both Lancaster's were hit on the bomb run, Garwells aircraft apparently being hit by an 88-mm gun sited on a flak tower, the fuselage erupting in a mass of flame behind the cockpit, but the aircraft continued on to release the 4 x 1,000 lb. bombs, two of which were noted to have fallen "slightly South of target and two in other section of area". Bombs gone, Garwells aircraft was in trouble, apparently being hit again after bomb release. The aircraft was afire, flames being evident from the fuselage as the aircraft was seen to make a forced landing by the crew of Nettleton's aircraft. Garwell crash landed the Lancaster in the only open space available, between the railway line and the water and uplands, three of the crew being killed. Garwell and the other three crew members got out of the aircraft, surrendering to a German civilian who had approached them on his bicycle.

Augsburg was now alerted when the second formation of six aircraft arrived several minutes after the attack by the two 44 Squadron Lancaster's. Like those of 44 Squadron, the aircraft of 97 Squadron had the main assembly hall as their aim point. Having crossed the French coast at 100 ft., flying at low level until the target was reached, No.97 Squadrons journey to Augsburg had been uneventful, although there is one claim that at least one of the 97 Squadron Lancaster's shot up a German train some 25 miles from Augsburg, but there is no mention of this in any of the operational records or reports to the War Cabinet and such an action would have flown in face of Bomber Command orders to attempt to reach the target without being discovered. Also, pre-mission the real concern was possible interception by enemy fighters on the homeward journey, therefore wasting precious ammunition on a train of absolutely no importance would seem to be an action less than prudent.

Flying in higher than the 44 Squadron aircraft, the 97 Squadron formation typically bombed at altitudes between 200 and 400 ft., visibility at the time being stated to be around 20 miles. Sherwood's vic attacked first. Sherwood's aircraft, L7573/K, released its bombs, but was trailing a stream of smoke as it left the target area, having been hit by flak. The crew of R5537/B noted that the anti-aircraft defences opened up when the aircraft was about two miles from the target. This aircraft released its bombs from 400 ft., the bombs probably "overshooting owing to aim being upset by shell in starboard wing." A large hole had been tore in the wing in the area of the main fuel tank. It was very shortly after this that the pilot had noticed white smoke coming from the port wing of Sherwood's aircraft. From the cockpit of R5488/F, "huge red flames" could be seen coming up from the target, anti-aircraft guns opening up as the aircraft entered the target area. The four 1,000 lb. bombs were dropped from an altitude of 200 ft., being noted "to burst on part of the works west of the canal."

As the first vic departed the target area crew from R5537/B and R5488/F noted increasing amounts of smoke or vapour coming from Sherwood's aircraft, which it was initially thought, or at least hoped, to be a fuel or coolant leak, but then the smoke turned black and a glow appeared in the area of the "inner petrol tank" dashing any such hopes as the aircraft caught fire, quickly turning into a conflagration. The aircraft began to decelerate, dropping back and losing altitude, allowing crew form another aircraft to see inside the stricken Lancaster through a burnt hatch; the scene described as being like a "blowtorch". The pilot of R5537/B instructed his rear gunner to keep the stricken Lancaster in view as long as possible, it being noted to hit the ground; the aircraft had crashed and exploded in woods several miles north of Augsburg. The crew were all killed except Sherwood who was apparently thrown through the windscreen, the branches of trees breaking his fall to earth, still strapped to his seat.

Trailing behind the first vic, the second vic, led by F/O. Penman in R5496/U, approached the target. This Aircraft dropped its bombs "in two sticks in centre of chimney clusters" from an altitude of 400 ft. L7575/Y dropped its bombs from 400 ft. This aircraft was hit on the starboard fuselage and bomb bay and caught fire, this being quickly extinguished by the Wireless Operator and Mid-Upper Gunner.

Some three miles out from the target R5513/P, flown by W/O. Mycock, was hit in the nose, the aircraft being set afire. Opting to stay on the bomb run rather than jettison bombs and climb to allow the crew to bail out, Mycock flew the Lancaster, now apparently with the port wing also afire, staying the course until the bombs were released in the target area following which the aircraft apparently climbed suddenly, going very close to Penman's aircraft which it apparently went over before diving and crashing into the ground in flames, all of the crew being killed.

Bombs gone, thoughts in the surviving aircraft turned to the return journey. Lancaster's R5537/B and R5488/F, flown by Hallows and Rodley respectively, withdrew together, keeping low until it started to get dark when they climbed to about 6,000 to 8,000 ft., and then, being separated, returned to base separately. On leaving the target area it was found that the mid-upper and rear gun turrets on L7575/Y had been rendered unserviceable and the outer port side engine was unserviceable, this being feathered for the return journey. With two of its gun turrets out of action, L7575/Y joined formation with R5496/U "for protection" on the journey home, its feathered engine being restarted again before the coast was reached.

All five surviving Lancaster's lumbering their way back across Germany and France had suffered varying degrees of damage. Luckily none were intercepted by German fighters on the homeward journey. R5496/U landed at Woodhall Spa at 22.57 hours, R5537/B landed at 23.12, L7575/Y landed at 23.15 and R5488/F landed at 23.25. The sole surviving 44 Squadron Lancaster, R5508/B, landed at Squires Gate near Blackpool at 00.50 hours on the morning of 18 April. The round distance covered by the 97 Squadron aircraft was in the order of 1,250 miles, the distance covered by the sole surviving 44 Squadron aircraft being around 1,500 miles. The exact route Nettleton took home has never been officially released. However, it is known that he crossed the English Channel and apparently flew across part of southern Britain, continuing out over the Irish Sea and then coming in to land at Squires Gate near Blackpool. It seems clear that there were some serious navigational issues in the aircraft, although what these were has not been publically revealed, even 73 years later. S/Ldr. Nettleton and his crew returned to Waddington later on the 18th, but Lancaster R5508/B remained at Squires Gate to have its wing examined.

Eight of the twelve Lancaster's dispatched had reached the target and dropped their bombs. Analysis later showed that seventeen of the thirty two bombs dropped had landed on target, although five of these had failed to explode. The bombs that detonated wrought carnage in "two machine-tool shops, a forging shop and the main assembly shop." However, the sheer size of the complex dictated that even if 48 bombs from the twelve Lancaster's dispatched had been on target and detonated the damage would not have been significant enough to cause serious disruption. At the time of the attack there were in the order of 2,700 machine tools in the factory, 3% of which were destroyed or damaged by the twelve bombs that hit the target and exploded, in addition of course to the damage to the buildings themselves. Other than that a number of cranes were damaged or destroyed, a bridge was damaged and a fair number of windows in Augsburg were smashed. This was a small return for the loss of seven Lancaster's and their crews, killed or captured, the production of the U-Boat engines barely pausing as a result of the raid. Twelve factory workers were also killed in the raid.

While there was much praise for the execution of the raid by the crews, behind the scenes there was much criticism for the choice of target for such an audacious undertaking, the cost of which, in both aircraft and crews, dictated could not be undertaken on a regular basis. Probably the most outspoken of the critics was Lord Selborne, head of the Ministry of Economic Warfare, who, in a letter to the Prime Minister, Winston Churchill, pointed out that Augsburg had been neither especially vulnerable to attack and was not even on the Ministry of Economic Warfare's "six classes of precise objective" most recommended for attack. He went on to point out that even if the factory at Augsburg had been "wiped out" German industry was still able to maintain the output of "ample diesel engine capacity". Lord Selborne went on to state that a target of far greater importance should have been selected for attack by Harris, and if he "had to operate near Augsburg there was always the great ball-bearing factory at Schweinfurt." Harris retorted that the factory at Augsburg was on the official list of targets whose destruction it was deemed would "greatly aid the struggle against the U-Boats". He also stated that Augsburg was selected as it was easy to recognise with easy to find landmarks such as Rivers which could be followed to the target area. Schweinfurt, he said, did not fit into this category.

Harris was supported by the Prime Minister, not least because the U-Boat menace, as would be recounted after the war, was Churchill's biggest cause of worry during the war. In early 1942, when the Augsburg raid was being planned, the U-boats were achieving enormous success. This period, known as the 'Second Happy Time' came about following the United States entry into the war; the Battle of the Atlantic had taken a turn for the worse, the U-Boats exploiting the easy pickings in their new killing grounds of the United States Eastern Seaboard.

Within 44 Squadron Nettleton was awarded a VC, the first South African VC of World War II. Garwell was awarded a DFC and his three surviving crew received DFM's. In 97 Squadron Sherwood and Penman received DSO's. In total there were nine DFC's to Officers and 13 DFM's to NCO's of both Squadrons. Sherwood had been recommended for the VC when it was thought he had been killed, but it was with a caveat that it was to be changed to a DSO if he was found to be alive. This left a bad taste in 97 Squadron ranks, however, the VC recommendation was the only way to ensure he was decorated in the event he was killed. If being shot down was the benchmark for being awarded a VC then 37 crew members would have been eligible, some of whom, perhaps, deserved a the award of a VC under its true requirement of gallantry above and beyond the call of duty. One such case was W/O. Mycock whose actions were certainly deserving of consideration for such an award. However, Mycock was apparently not even recommended by his CO, his actions going unrecognised as far as honors go. Another case would have been Garwell and his crew who continued on through hundreds of miles of enemy territory with cannon damage to one of the Lancaster's wings after the action with the German fighters over Normandy. Unfortunately there was no posthumous award in 1942 other than the VC, therefore, the crew members from both squadrons who lost their lives on the raid received were not decorated.

Narrative concerning Nettleton's Aircraft:

Primary target attacked – M.A.N. Diesel Engine Factory at Augsburg. Time 19.55 hours. Height 50 feet. Bombs 4 x 1,000 lbs. dropped in target area. Bombs seen to burst by rear gunner, and Captain on turning aircraft. Two of F.O Garwells bombs seen to fall slightly south of target and two in other section of area. Pilot states:- Set course for Selsey Bill at low level and whole trip done at low level until it became too dark on return. After setting course from Selsey Bill it was noticed that grooves appeared in the main planes about 2 or 3 inches wide just outboard of the inboard engines on both sides. Ten minutes after crossing the coast (French) fighters were encountered and attacked the formation in the vicinity of BERNEY. On reaching the target light flak was intense and accurate, but heavy flak most inaccurate. F/O Garwell in 'A' of 44 was hit and caught fire. He made what appeared a successful forced landing and it is thought that all the crew would have most probably been safe. During the fighters attack the rear guns seized after firing approx. 800 rounds. The return journey was uneventful. Three aircraft including 'H' (Capt. Sgt. Rhodes) of 44 Squadron were seen to crash and another on fire. Time off 15.12. Time in 00.50 at Squires Gate.

The 44 Squadron Narrative of the Operation read:

Operations. An operation was detailed to be carried out with No.97 Squadron as follows:

Six aircraft from each Squadron loaded with four 1000 G.P. bombs to take off at 15.15 hours to bomb the M.A.N. Diesel Engine Factory at Augsburg. Each Squadron flying in formations of two sections of three would proceed to the target without fighter escort via Selsey Bill – Villers-Sur-Mer – Sans –Ludwigshaven on Lake Konstang – Amer See and thence North to Augsburg. No fighter escort would be provided but diversionary raids would be staged in the Pas de Calais, Cherbourg and Rouen areas by fighters and bombers commencing fifty minutes before aircraft were due to cross the French Coast so that enemy fighters, in addition to being kept fully employed, would require to re-fuel and re-arm before being able to intercept.

The first Section of three (led by S/Ldr. Nettleton with F/O Garwell, DFM, and Sgt. Rhodes) took off at 15.12 hours followed by the second section at 15.14 hours (leader F/Lt. Sandford with W/O Beckett, DFM and W/O Crum, DFM) and set course for Selsey Bill. The French Coast was crossed at 16.45 hours and at 16.55 hours both formations were intercepted by between twenty-five and thirty fighters and a running fight ensued as a result of which Sgt. Rhodes (Aircraft No. L.7536.H.) was firstly shot down followed by all three aircraft of the second formation (F/Lt. Sandford – Aircraft No. R.5506.P, W/O Crum, DFM – Aircraft No. L7548.T, W.O. Beckett, DFM – Aircraft No. L.7565.V.). This engagement lasted until 17.55 hours and the two remaining aircraft S/Ldr. Nettleton and F.O. Garwell, DFM) continued their journey at "tree-top" height until the target was reached at 19.55 hours.

The target was approached from Lake Ammer by both remaining aircraft at "tree-top" height. The Munich-Augsburg Railway line was crossed at Mering and, although the intention was to fly direct to the target, it was decided otherwise owing to the number of chimney stacks which would necessitate an unnecessary increase in height. The river Lech was accordingly followed and the attack was made from an Easterly direction. Both aircraft dropped their bombs which were seen by the rear gunner of the Leader's aircraft to hit the factory buildings. As the bombs were released the Ground Defences opened up and violent evasive action to the South was taken during which Sergeant Huntly silenced one of the main defensive gun posts with his guns. The bombs had eleven seconds delay and the explosions from them were observed by Pilots and Gunners. Whole sections of the buildings were blasted into the air. At this time F/O. Garwell's aircraft broke formation and increased its height. It was noticed that the aircraft was on fire (it had previously been shot up in the action with the enemy fighters). The aircraft was then seen to make a forced-landing in some fields two miles to the West of the Town. The tail section was seen to break away from the centre turret.

Thereafter the one and only remaining aircraft of this Squadron's formation set course for "base" and eventually landed at Squires Gate at 00.55 hours on 18th April.

Note: This account, like that of the official history states the action with the fighters lasted a full hour, but other evidence from Nettleton's aircraft, including the Combat Report, and evidence from German records make it clear that the combat lasted between ten and fifteen minutes, certainly not much longer. In addition, the above account states that Sgt. Rhodes aircraft, in the first vic, was the first Lancaster shot down, but other accounts suggest that Rhodes aircraft was the last of the four Lancaster's to be shot down by the German fighters.

The Official Air Ministry Narrative of the operation read:

(No.346 – Part.).
The main target during daylight hours was the M.A.N. Meschinen
fabric Augsburg Nurnberg A.G. at Augsburg. This most important works
is the largest Diesel Engine Factory in Germany producing half the total
requirements for large submarines as well as engines for warships, tanks
and Lorries. The attack was made by twelve Lancaster's involving a
journey of some 1,250 miles, chiefly over Enemy territory. A large
diversionary effort was made by 30 Boston's and nearly 800 Fighter
Aircraft in the Pas de Calais, Cherbourg and Rouen areas.
AUGSBURG   Eight Lancaster's attacked in good weather and
visibility at about 20.15 hours from 200 to 300 feet and dropped 32 x 1000
lb. Bombs. Crews report explosions and flames in the target area. Very
heavy flak was experienced and one of the Lancaster's going in to attack
was hit, but continued dropped his bombs and was then seen to force-
land in flames near the target. There was no opposition from ground
defences on the way out or back but some Enemy fighters were
encountered in the Barney area. Seven Lancaster's failed to return.

Note: The above account implies that all eight Lancaster's that bombed the
target did so in concert, however, we know form operational records on both
sides that this was not the case. The account also states that the time of the
attack was 20.15 hours, but we know from Nettleton's account and German
records that the time of the first attack was around 19.55 hours. The account
only mentions one Lancaster shot down over the target whereas the actual
number was three, one from the 44 Squadron formation and two from the 97
Squadron formation.

Following the raid messages poured in from various high ranking sources.
This message from the Prime Minister to the Air Officer Commander-in-
Chief, Bomber Command was passed on to the Squadrons:

The Prime Minister:-
    "We must plainly regard the attack of the Lancaster's on the U-
Boat Engine Factory at Augsburg as an outstanding achievement of the
Royal Air Force. Undeterred by heavy losses at the outset 44 and 97
Squadrons pierced in broad daylight into the heart of Germany and
struck a vital point with deadly precision. Pray convey the thanks of His
Majesty's Government to the Officers and men who accomplished this
memorable feat of arms in which no life was lost in vain."

Air Marshall A.T. Harris., C.B., O.B.E., A.F.C., Commander-in-Chief Bomber Command, sent the following message:-

**"Convey to the crews of 44 and 97 Squadrons who took part in the Augsburg raid the following: The resounding blow which has been struck at the enemy's submarine and tank building program will echo round the world. The full effects of his submarine campaign cannot be immediately apparent, but nevertheless they will be enormous. The gallant adventure penetrating deep into the heart of Germany in daylight and pressed with outstanding determination in the face of bitter and foreseen opposition takes its place amongst the most courageous operations of the war. It is, moreover, yet another example of effective co-operation with the other services by striking at the very source of enemy effort. The Officers and men who took part, those who returned and those who fell, have indeed deserved well of their Country."**

While some of these messages, politically motivated perhaps, gave the impression that a the plant had suffered vast amounts of damage severely affecting diesel engine output and thus Germany's ability to wage her Submarine campaign with the same level of effectiveness as before, behind closed doors there can be no doubt that within the British establishment the reality of the situation was clear. Whatever level of damage inflicted, the Submarine campaign would go on as before.

The following is an extract form the Augsburg Raid Assessment Report obtained through photographs taken by a Photographic Reconnaissance mission on 29 April 1942:

*Augsburg* – Photographs taken on 29th April show the following damage resulting from the raid on 17th April:-
(a) The main Diesel Engine Shops of 1-3 storeys and covering an area of 20,000 square yards are severely damaged by a number of direct hits, and there is probable fire damage to a top storey.
(b) Roof damage to two small buildings and a workshop.
(c) A large building, probably connected with the power station, is demolished and others badly damaged by blast.
(d) Out of four buildings believed to be stores for machine parts, two are demolished and two damaged.
(e) Several workshops and weaving sheds outside the main target area are damaged, one seriously.

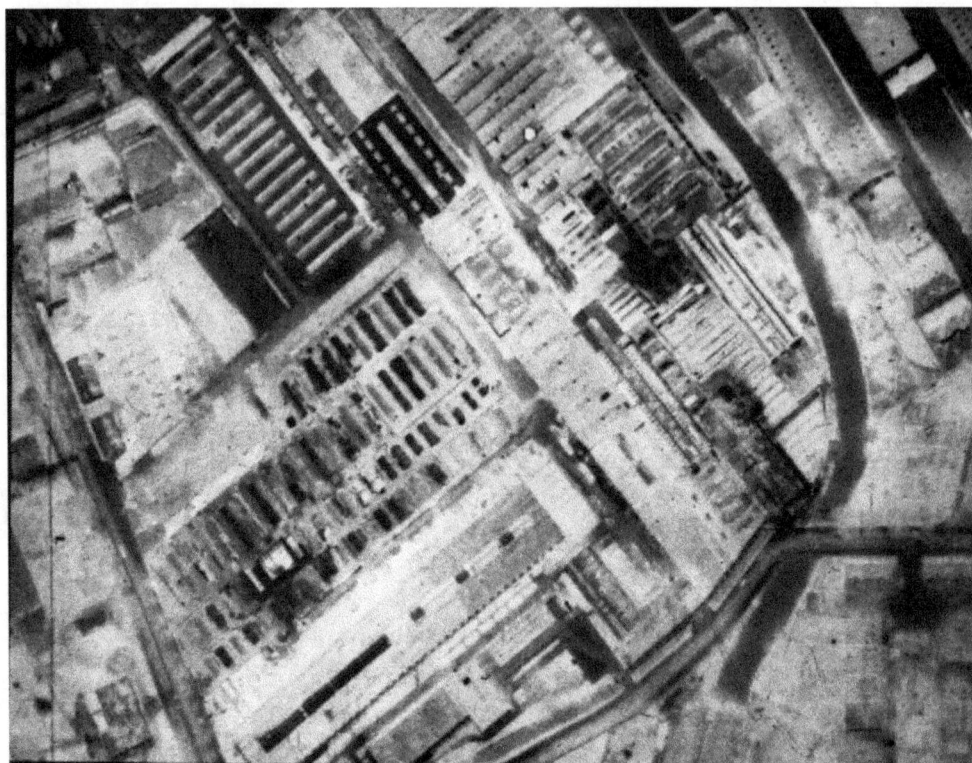

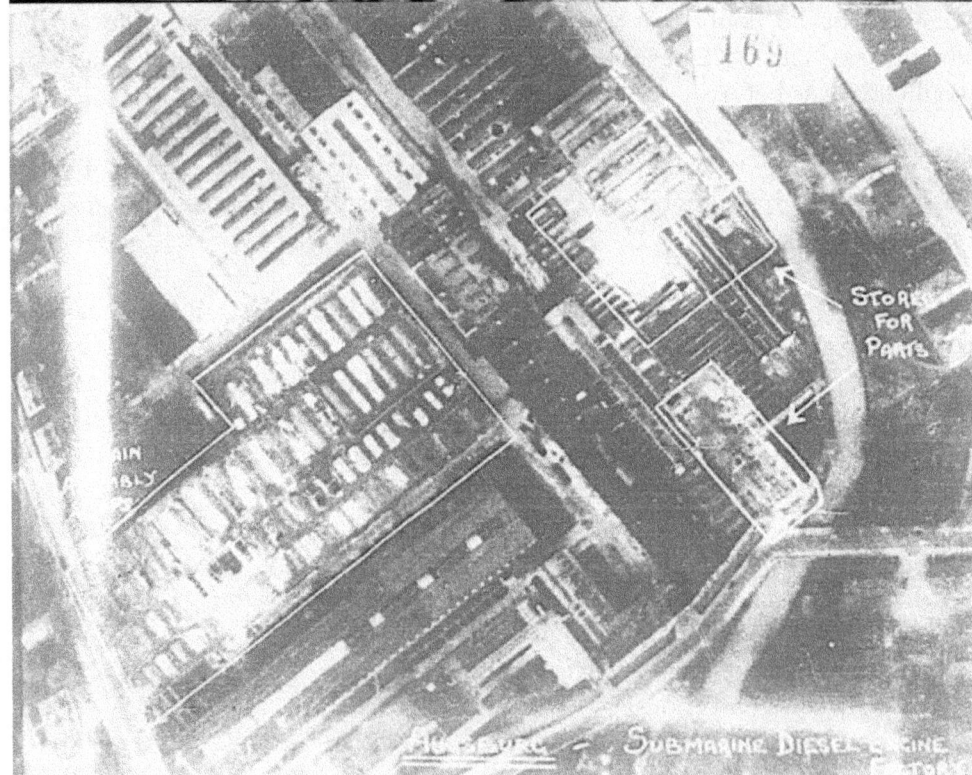

AUGSBURG — SUBMARINE DIESEL ENGINE

STORES FOR PARTS

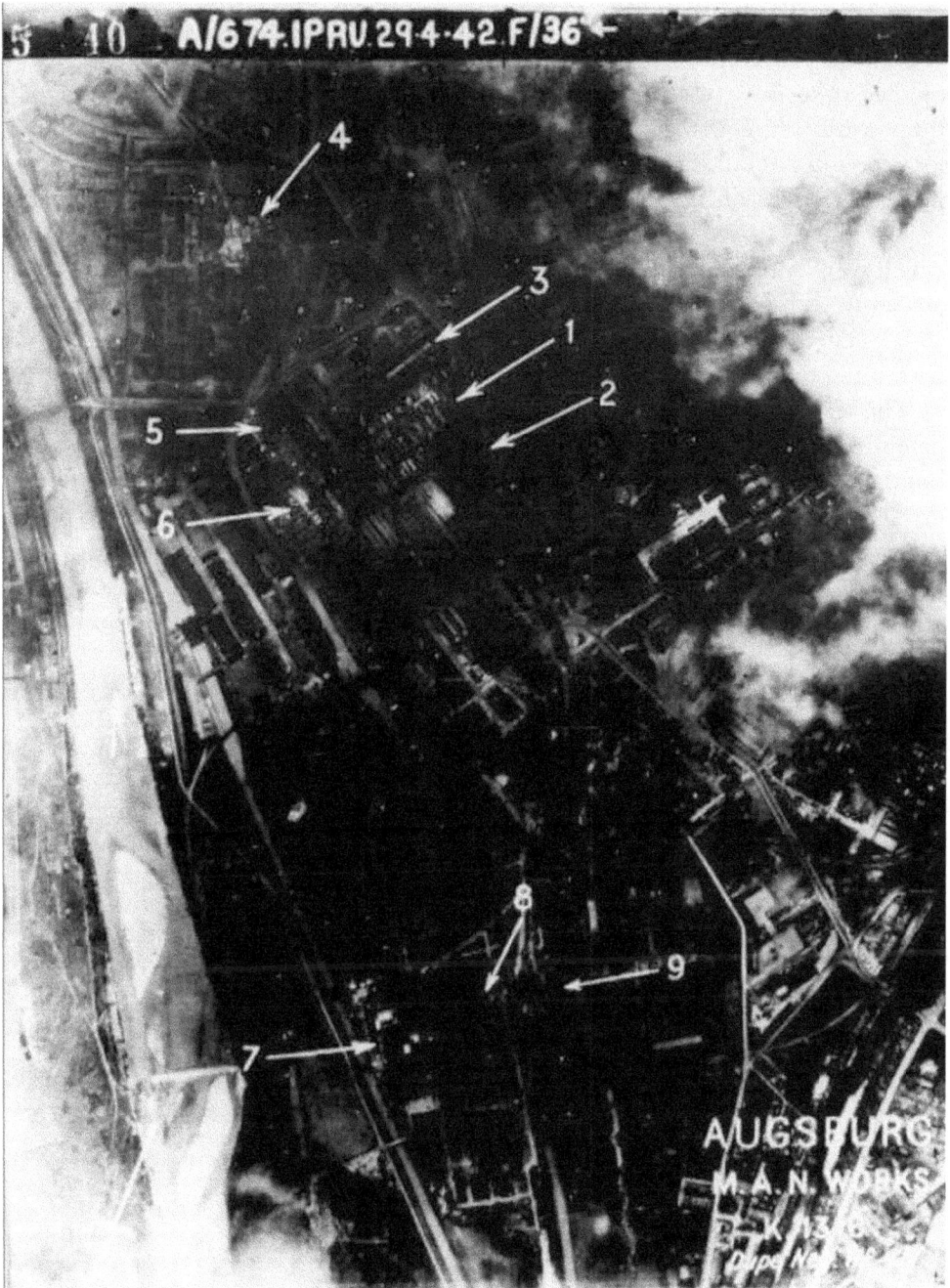

Bomb damage assessment photographs of the MAN factory were taken by a photographic reconnaissance aircraft on 29 April 1942. The images on the previous page are similar, the bottom one showing the position of damaged stores buildings. The image above shows the position of nine of the bomb hits.

There can be no doubt that the Augsburg raid was a success in terms of the target being accurately bombed, but this was achieved at a very high cost, 58.5% of the strike force was lost, and of the eight aircraft that bombed the target, three were lost, equating to 37.5% of the aircraft that reached the target being lost to anti-aircraft fire. The small amount of damage caused, with only a negligible effect on diesel engine output, had virtually no effect on the battle against the U-Boats; a small return for the loss of seven valuable Lancaster's which were sorely needed by Bomber Command. The modern Lancaster's "had got away with it little better than the Wellingtons in 1940 or the Blenheim's in 1941" stated the official history. Thirty seven of the eighty five crew who took part in the raid were killed and twelve taken prisoner.

The raid, however, did show that Bomber Command could strike at defended targets in the heart of Germany in broad daylight using its new heavy bombers. However, any hopes that the Germans would divert significant fighter units from the Eastern Front, thereby aiding the Soviet Union in its titanic struggle against the bulk of the German war machine, were forlorn, for the German High Command knew, as did the British, that Bomber Command could not mount such raids on any increased scale or frequency in the face of such losses.

# 3

# POSTSCRIPT

As mentioned above, among the lessons learned from the Augsburg raid was that daylight raids into the heart of Germany could only be accomplished at great cost. It was clear that losses over the target would probably be lighter if the aircraft flew at altitudes of 15-20,000 ft., but this would have come at the unacceptable price of vastly reduced accuracy and increased vulnerability to German fighters. Post Augsburg, Bomber Command continued to fly limited numbers of daylight raids utilising its heavy bombers, but attacks deep into Germany were now considered too costly. Later in 1942, when the high speed de Havilland Mosquito became available to Bomber Command, further small scale daylight raids into the heart of Germany were conducted, usually by single aircraft using cloud as cover and high speed for protection.

The Lancaster's war, however, had only just begun and the aircraft would be employed extensively in the night bombing campaign as increasing numbers of Squadrons received the aircraft. Daylight raids would also be conducted, particularly later in the war, and the aircraft was used by No.617 Squadron in the raids on the German Dams in May 1943 and attacks on the Battleship Tirpitz which capsized after being attacked with Lancaster's armed with 12,000 lb. Tallboy bombs on 12 November 1944.

As for Augsburg, as the war progressed it would, unfortunately, suffer a fate suffered by so many German towns and City's, being devastated in a series of day and night attacks such as those of 25/26 February 1944 when 194 USAAF B-17 Flying Fortress bombers dropped 481 tons of bombs during the day on the 25th, this being followed up that night by several hundred RAF heavy bombers dropping a proportionately greater tonnage of bombs, the target for both raids being aircraft assembly plants, but the town of Augsburg itself being devastated with huge loss of life among the civil population.

No.617 Squadron, colloquially known as the 'Dam Busters' following their audacious raid on the German Dams in the Ruhr in May 1943, operated heavily modified Lancaster B MK.I Bombers known s B MK.I (Special). These aircraft carried the massive 22,000 lb. 'Grand Slam', deep penetration bomb, the so called 'earthquake bomb' which were used to devastating effect in a number of missions in the last months of the war. The smaller 12,000 lb. Tallboy bomb was also operated by 617 Squadron, this weapon being used to sink the German Battleship Tirpitz when the vessel capsized after being hit by one of the weapons in November 1944.

Previous page top: This Lancaster B MK.I (Special) at Woodhall Spa is carrying a 22,000lb. Grand Slam in the specially modified recess in the aircraft's underside. Previous page bottom: This B MK.I (Special) has just released a 'Grand Slam' during No.617 Squadrons attack on the viaduct at Arnsberg, Germany on 19 March 1945. RAF

This page: The Lancaster MK.I became the stalwart of Bomber Command, augmented by other Models including the B MK.III, which was basically a B MK.I powered by US built Packard Merlin 28 engines. The prototype Lancaster B MK.III, W4114, here at the A&AEE Bascombe Down, Wiltshire, was converted from a standard BMK.I. MAP

# APPENDICES

## Appendix I

The following is taken from the Air Ministry performance card for Lancaster I and III aircraft, dated 12.2.1945

WEIGHTS

| | |
|---|---|
| Maximum lb. | 68,000 |
| Mean lb. | 55,000 |
| Light lb. oil | |
| (No fuel oil/Bombs) | 41,000 |
| Tare lb. | 36,900 |

DIMENSIONS

| | |
|---|---|
| Span ft. | 102 |
| Gross wing area sq. ft. | 1,297 |
| Length ft. | 68.9 |
| Height ft. (Tail-down) | 19.5 |
| Crew | 7 |

PERFORMANCE.

| | |
|---|---|
| Take-off over 50 ft. (Max wt.) yards | 1,500 |
| (at 45,000 lb.) yards | 1,200 |
| Landing over 50 ft. yards | 1,000 |
| Service ceiling (Max wt.) ft. | 20,000 |
| Service ceiling (Mean wt.) ft. | |
| Maximum speed at 64,500 lb. m.p.h | 271 |
| Maximum speed at optimum weight m.p.h | 281 (at combat power) |
| Cruising speed at 20,000 ft. | |
| (most economical m.p.h at Mean weight) | 216 |
| At maximum weak mixture power m.p.h. | 227 |
| TIME TO 20,000 ft. (max weight) minutes | 41.6 |

ARMAMENT.
GUNS.

| | | |
|---|---|---|
| Bore | .303 in | |
| No. | 2 Turret Nose | 1,000 Rds/Gun |
| | 4 Turret Tail | 2,500 Rds/Gun |
| | 2 Top Body | 1,000 Rds/Gun |
| | Under | |

MAXIMUM ALTERNATIVE BOMB LOADS.

| Fuselage lbs. | Total lb. |
|---|---|
| 14 x 1,000 lb. (Special) | 14,000 |
| 6 x 2,000 lb., plus 3 x 250 lb. | 12,750 |
| 6 x 500 lb. Mines | 9,000 |
| 1 x 8,000 lb. | 8,000 |
| 1 x 4,000 lb. plus 6 x 500 lb. | 7,000 |
| 14 x 500lb. | 7,000 |

RANGE –BOMB LOAD TABLE
(at most economical speed)

| | Max bombs | Perm Tanks | Aux. Tank | Two Aux Tanks |
|---|---|---|---|---|
| Fuel carried gall. | 1,625 | 2,150 | 2,550 | 2,950 |
| Fuel Allowance gall. | 270 | 270 | 270 | 270 |
| Range miles | 1,660 | 2,250 | 2,680 | 3,150 |
| Bombs carried lb. | 14,000 | 10,000 | 7,000 | - |

Engines  Merlin 22, 28 & 38
No. 4
Power (max) b.h.p.          M.  1,460    S.   1,435

Note: The early production Lancaster MK.I's involved in the Augsburg raid were powered by Rolls Royce Merlin XX engines, however, the performance differences from those stated above would have been negligible.

## Appendix II

Lancaster MK I Bombers that participated in the Augsburg raid

44 Squadron

| | | |
|---|---|---|
| R5508/B | Damaged | AA over Target |
| R5510/A | Lost | Shot down by AA over target |
| L7536/H | Lost | Shot down by fighters over France |
| L7565/V | Lost | Shot down by fighters over France |
| R5506/P | Lost | Shot down by fighters over France |
| L7548/T | Lost | Shot down by fighters over France |

97 Squadron

| | | |
|---|---|---|
| L7573/K | Lost | Shot down by AA over target |
| R5537/B | Damaged | AA over target |
| R5488/F | Damaged | AA over target |
| R5496/U | Damaged | AA over target |
| L7575/Y | Damaged | AA over target |
| R5513/P | Lost | Shot down by AA over target |

At least one of the 97 Squadron aircraft, apparently R5537/B, was written off after its return from the Augsburg raid, bringing to eight, the cost in Lancaster's for Operation Margin

# GLOSSARY

| | |
|---|---|
| AA | Anti-Aircraft |
| A&AEE | Aeroplane and Armament Experimental Establishment |
| BC | Bomber Command |
| BO | British Official |
| ESE | East South East |
| F/Lt | Flight Lieutenant |
| F/O | Flying Officer |
| F/Sgt | Flight Sergeant |
| FW | Focke Wulf |
| Gall | Gallon |
| Hrs. | Hours |
| I | One |
| IAS | Indicated Air Speed |
| Lb. | pound |
| III | Three |
| IV | Four |
| MAN | Maschinenfabrik Augsburg Nürnberg |
| ME | Messerschmitt |
| MOI | Ministry Of Information |
| MPH | Miles Per Hour |
| No | Number |
| P/O | Pilot Officer |
| RAF | Royal Air Force |
| S/Ldr | Squadron Leader |
| WNW | West North West |
| W/O | Warrant Officer |
| X | Ten |
| XX | Twenty |
| Yds. | Yards |

# BIBLIOGRAPHY

Primary documents consulted in preparation of this volume:

No.44 Squadron Operations Record Book Form 540, April 1942
No.44 Squadron Operations Record Book Form 541, April 1942
No.97 Squadron Operations Record Book Form 540 April 1942
No.97 Squadron Operations Record Book Form 541 April 1942
No.44 Squadron Combat Report for 17 April 1942
No.44 Squadron Narrative of the Augsburg Operation
Air Ministry Narrative of the Augsburg Operation
W.P. (42) 176. Memorandum for the War Cabinet, April 23, 1942
W.P. (42) 194. Memorandum for the War Cabinet, May 7, 1942
W.P. (42) 204. War Cabinet, Summary of Operations of Bomber Command for
Fortnight Ending 1200 Hours Sunday, May 10, 1942
Augsburg Raid Assessment Report
History of the Second World War, The RAF 1939-45 Volume II, 1953, HMSO
Message from the Prime Minister to the Air Officer Commander-in-Chief,
Bomber Command
Message to 44 and 97 Squadrons from Air Marshall A.T. Harris., C.B., O.B.E.,
A.F.C., Commander-in-Chief Bomber Command
    In addition several hundred miscellaneous pages of documents;
development, operational, command and political were consulted

# ABOUT THE AUTHOR

Hugh, a historian and author, has published in excess of forty books; non-fiction and fiction, writing under his given name as well as utilising two different pseudonyms. He has also written for several international magazines, whilst his work has been used as reference for many other projects ranging from the aviation industry, international news corporations and film media to encyclopedias, museum exhibits and the computer gaming industry. He currently resides in his native Scotland

Other titles by the Author include

Hurricane IIB Combat Log - 151 Wing RAF, North Russia 1941
RAF Meteor Jet Fighters in World War II, an Operational Log
Typhoon IA/B Combat Log - Operation Jubilee, August 1942
Defiant MK.I Combat Log - Fighter Command, May-September 1940
Blenheim MK.IF Combat Log - Fighter Command Day Fighter Sweeps/Night Interceptions - September 1939 - June 1941
Tomahawk I/II Combat Log - European Theatre - 1941-42
Fortress MK.I Combat Log – Bomber Command High Altitude Bombing Operations, July-September 1941
Eurofighter Typhoon - Storm over Europe
Tornado F.2/F.3 Air Defence Variant
Air to Air Missile Directory
British Battlecruisers of World War 1 - Operational Log, July 1914-June 1915
Light Battle Cruisers and the Second Battle of Heligoland Bight
Boeing X-36 Tailless Agility Flight Research Aircraft
X-32 - The Boeing Joint Strike Fighter
X-35 - Progenitor to the F-35 Lightning II
X-45 Uninhabited Combat Air Vehicle
North American F-108 Rapier
Sukhoi Su-34 'Fullback' - Russia's 21st Century Striker
F-84 Thunderjet - Republic Thunder
USAF Jet Powered Fighters - XP-59-XF-85
XF-92 - Convairs Arrow
Saab Gripen, The Nordic Myth
Dassault Rafale, The Gallic Squall

www.ingramcontent.com/pod-product-compliance
Lightning Source LLC
LaVergne TN
LVHW061328060426
835511LV00012B/1918